T0375534

You Are Not Alone in Your Loss

Inspirational Words to Work You Through Grief

DORIS OYINLOYE

WESTBOW
P R E S S®
A DIVISION OF THOMAS NELSON
& ZONDERVAN

Copyright © 2024 Doris Oyinloye.

All rights reserved. No part of this book may be used or reproduced by any means, graphic, electronic, or mechanical, including photocopying, recording, taping or by any information storage retrieval system without the written permission of the author except in the case of brief quotations embodied in critical articles and reviews.

This book is a work of non-fiction. Unless otherwise noted, the author and the publisher make no explicit guarantees as to the accuracy of the information contained in this book and in some cases, names of people and places have been altered to protect their privacy.

WestBow Press books may be ordered through booksellers or by contacting:

WestBow Press
A Division of Thomas Nelson & Zondervan
1663 Liberty Drive
Bloomington, IN 47403
www.westbowpress.com
844-714-3454

Because of the dynamic nature of the Internet, any web addresses or links contained in this book may have changed since publication and may no longer be valid. The views expressed in this work are solely those of the author and do not necessarily reflect the views of the publisher, and the publisher hereby disclaims any responsibility for them.

Any people depicted in stock imagery provided by Getty Images are models, and such images are being used for illustrative purposes only.
Certain stock imagery © Getty Images.

Scripture quotations are taken from the New King James Version. Copyright © 1982 by Thomas Nelson, Inc. Used by permission. All rights reserved.

ISBN: 979-8-3850-1680-8 (sc)
ISBN: 979-8-3850-1681-5 (e)

Library of Congress Control Number: 2024900737

Print information available on the last page.

WestBow Press rev. date: 02/21/2024

Contents

Dedication

A huge debt of gratitude goes to almighty God, the Creator of heaven and the earth. His words become the rock of my strength and hope. He loved me when I was unlovable. He gave His life for me when there was no reason to do so.

To my late mother, Sabainah Ajike, and my hero, I will ever be grateful for the Christian virtues you instilled in me, the strongest tool in my life's journey—she taught me not only to cope but to grow and to believe in the top of the mountain even when I can't see it.

Life's meaning also comes from the special people around me. Professor, Doctor, and Pastor Joseph A. Ola is part of my faith journey. With his unconditional and unwavering spiritual support and inspirational messages when I needed it most after the death of my husband, Zacchaeus Adebayo Oyinloye. Pastor Ola gave me the courage for the long haul and encouraged me for each day's journey.

Introduction

My life as a second child of twenty-two siblings was heavily affected by experiencing loss and grief on all levels. I was born into a polygamous family of one mother and a famous father, who had four wives. It was a mixed family filled with some joy, happiness, turbulent crises, and sibling rivalry, which grew like a planted weed.

It was a home where every day was a struggle for survival. Life was like a nightmare for my mother and her six children. There were feelings of fear, hate, jealousy, and insecurity. At three years old, I became a caregiver to my twin brothers, who were born with post-birth complications, which kept my mother in the hospital and away from her babies for several months. I was left to face the role of motherhood at that tender age along with my grandmother.

Both of my parents passed away too soon. Then came the mysterious, sudden death of my sister, brother, and husband. He was my best friend, and the father of our four children, who emerged as a kind and sensitive adult.

The more sudden the death was, the longer it took to grieve the loss. My world turned upside down without my parents and husband. It was too hard for me to view all these losses as only a rite of passage. For me, it was difficult to process the feelings during the onset of the situation. The only way out was going through the pain and letting myself feel it, mourn it, and move on. In my loneliness and sorrow, I believed the world held me in its embrace. When I felt alone because of little or no family gatherings, lonely holidays, no Father's Days, and being unsure of my purpose, feeling insecure about who I was, and underappreciated for what I did, God's words and His promises assured me.

Fear not, for I am with you; Be not dismayed, for I am your God. I will strengthen you, yes, I will help you, I will uphold you with My righteous right hand. (Isaiah 41:10)

Because of God's Word and promises, I'm His masterpiece, I'm known and loved, and I lack nothing. There would be something missing in creation without me! I believe that I'm

A chosen generation, a royal priesthood, a holy nation, His own special people, that I may proclaim the praises of Him who called me out of darkness into His marvelous light; who once were not a people but are now the people of God, who had not obtained mercy but now have obtained mercy. (1 Peter 2:9–10)

It feels so sweet to trust in Jesus and just rest upon His words and promises. My only task is to ask for His grace to trust Him more and daily.

My losses shifted the ground beneath me just as a landslide or an earthquake does. Each loss was longer and more painful. But in my weakness, I turned and put my hope and trust in the only One who was strong and who promised hope, God almighty.

Although my mother's life was cut short at age fifty-two, she spent her life preparing her six children for the future we were to face. She instilled in us honesty, perseverance, faith in the Lord, resiliency, and what it took to face life's challenges. I will ever be grateful for these gifts, which have withstood the tests of my life. Those Christian virtues prepared me for hardships, fears, failures, and the exposures that came in my life's journey. It made me who I am today—a health-care giver, which is a kind, loving, compassionate, and caring profession.

We all have a moment in our lives when we have to go through losses, griefs, and mourning, but our journey through it either makes us or breaks us. We all need the resources to help us through this dark road. A time of sorrow takes up the whole landscape, but joy will come again. Don't go through your pain but grow through it. Turn your grief and pain into a new hope to help others through theirs. There is a purpose for your loss.

As you hold this book, remember you are never alone in your loss. God is always very near and close to you in your journey. The problems of the world around you can be frightening, but God is greater than your problems. Count on Him because He is perfect, and His plans are good. His power is perfected in your weakness, and it is greater than any situation you might face.

Chapter 1

GOD'S UNLIMITED RESOURCES

When you feel tired, overwhelmed, discouraged, helpless, hopeless, or completely shattered, you are not alone. God's resources are unlimited. His words are authentic and everlasting. The possibilities are endless. And He specializes in making all things new. That is the character of the King of kings and the Lord of lords, Jesus, our Savior.

> Our help is in the name of the LORD, who made heaven
> and earth. (Psalm 124:8)

I pray that from His glorious, unlimited resources, He will empower you with inner strength through His Spirit. I pray that God, the Source of hope, will fill you completely with joy and peace because you trust in Him. May you overflow with confidence and hope through the power of the Holy Spirit. Amen.

"God Will Take Care of You" is a song by Walter Stillman Martin. [A1]

> Be not dismayed whatever betide, God will take care of
> you; Beneath His wings of love abide, God will take care
> of you.

Through days of toil when your heart doth fail, God will take care of you; When dangers fierce your path assail, God will take care of you.

All you may need He will provide; God will take care of you; Nothing you ask will be denied, God will take care of you.

No matter what may be the test, God will take care of you; Lean, weary one, upon His breast, God will take care of you.

God will take care, through every day, o'er all the way; He will take care of you, God will take care of you."

Our society places enormous pressure on us to get over loss. But how long do you grieve for your loved ones? The answer is simple: You grieve as long as you need to. Real grief is not healed by time. The loss of loved ones is excruciating. Some losses are unexpected and shocking, leaving you unprepared and unable to say goodbye. This makes the denial and grieving process longer and deeper. Most nights become long, too quiet, lonely, and difficult. When the telephone doesn't ring, the longing and the torment of having to get through another night of grief becomes a nightmare.

Grief is a time to be lived through and experienced fully because when our loved ones die, something in us dies too—some expectation or hope of a future together. And out of the ashes of that destroyed dream, we have been lifted into new life. Heaven will not fall if you give voice to your anger against God in such a time because anger is part of your grief.

We are all weighed down with burdens that only Jesus can remove. He knows the weakness of humanity (our wants and the strength of our temptations). Whatever our anxieties and trials are, Jesus invites us to spread them out before Him. Fear, pain, and losses can serve two purposes: They either paralyze a person into doing nothing or motivate person to take action to overcome it.

Henri Nouwen said, [A2]

> "When I trust deeply that today God is truly with me
> and holds me safe in a divine embrace, guiding every one
> of my steps I can let go of my anxious need to know how
> tomorrow will look, or what will happen next month or
> next year. I can be fully where I am and pay attention to
> the many signs of God's love within me and around me."

> God's promises include: I have called you by name from
> the very beginning. You are mine and I am yours. You are
> my Beloved, on you my favor rests. I have molded you in
> the depth of the earth and knitted you together in your
> mother's womb. I have carved you in the palms of my
> hands and hidden you in the shadow of my embrace. I
> look at you with infinite tenderness and care for you with
> a care more intimate than that of a mother for her child.
> I have counted every hair on your head and guided you
> at every step.

Henri Nouwen's *Life of the Beloved* echoes our heavenly Father's
promise for us.

> "Wherever you go, I go with you, and whenever you rest,
> I keep watch. I will give you food that will satisfy all your
> hunger and drink that will quench all your thirst. I will
> not hide my face from you. You know me as your own
> as I know you as my own. You belong to me, I am your
> father, your mother, your brother, your sister, your lover
> and your spouse … yes, even your child … wherever you
> are I will be. Nothing will ever separate us. We are one".

Therefore, "we do not look at the things which are seen, but at the
things which are not seen. For the things which are seen are temporary,
but the things which are not seen are eternal" (2 Corinthians 4:18).

Turn your eyes upon Jesus, look full in His wonderful face; and the things of the earth will grow strangely dim in the light of his glory and grace.

When we walk with the Lord in the light of His word, what a glory He sheds on our way, while we do His good will, He abides with us still, and with all who will trust and obey.

Trust and obey, for there is no other way to be happy in Jesus, but to trust and obey.

Chapter 2

GOD'S WORD FOR STRENGTH

It is never easy to say goodbye to a loved one. We must allow ourselves to be interrupted by God. His ways are not our ways. We must accept His answers to our prayers in His mysterious and divine way. We may ask for strength and may have difficulties to make us strong. We may ask for wisdom and may have problems to solve. We may ask for courage and may have dangers to overcome. We may also ask for love and may have troubled people to help. Our prayers are still answered in God's way.

God is our refuge and strength, a very present help in trouble. Therefore, we will not fear, even though the earth be removed, and though the mountains be carried into the midst of the sea; Though its waters roar and be troubled, though the mountains shake with its swelling.
(Psalm 46:1–3)

As for man, his days are like grass; As a flower of the field, so he flourishes. For the wind passes over it, and it is gone, and its place remembers it no more. But the mercy of the Lord is from everlasting to everlasting on those who fear Him, and His righteousness to children's children.
(Psalm 103:15–17)

Sometimes to make it through the night to the next morning is fearful and difficult, especially when alone. It is then things are quiet and the telephone doesn't ring, the loneliness sets in, but still remember to be grateful from the core of your being for the life you have shared with your loved one. Learn to trust the turning of the seasons, the season that support you in your journey through grief. Some people come into our lives and quickly go! Some people stay for a while and leave footprints on our hearts; we are never the same. Sometimes you found that your circle of friends shifted ... you were surprised and disappointed that people you thought were good friends become distant, uneasy, and seemed unable to help you. Others who were casual acquaintances became suddenly close, sustainers of life for us. Grief changes the rules, and sometimes rearranges the combinations.

> I would have lost heart, unless I had believed that I would see the goodness of the Lord in the land of the living. Wait on the Lord; be of good courage, and He shall strengthen your heart; wait, I say, on the Lord! (Psalm 27:13–14)

If you stay true to God when you are under the fire of trials, you will give God the opportunity to show you His power. We have this hope by grace.

> For the eyes of the LORD run to and fro throughout the whole earth, to show Himself strong on behalf of those whose heart *is* loyal to Him. (2 Chronicles 16:9)

God will answer your secret prayers. He will wipe away your secret tears and lift you to the position you secretly desire. Your victory is sure in Him.

> But you, when you pray, go into your room, and when you have shut your door, pray to your Father who *is* in the secret place; and your Father who sees in secret will reward you openly. (Matthew 6:6)

You will overcome your trials because the God of grace is your refuge in adversity and times of storms. The power that calmed the storming sea is still alive to calm your life's troubles. He rebuked the wind and storm, and it stood still. He will still all the storms in your life because in Him, your victory is sure.

> Now when He got into a boat, His disciples followed Him. And suddenly a great tempest arose on the sea, so that the boat was covered with the waves. But He was asleep. Then His disciples came to Him and awoke Him, saying, "Lord, save us! We are perishing!" But He said to them, "Why are you fearful, O you of little faith?" Then He arose and rebuked the winds and the sea, and there was a great calm. So the men marveled, saying, "Who can this be, that even the winds and the sea obey Him?" (Luke 8:23–27)

When you call on Jesus in times of trouble, He will never fail you. Believe and try Him now.

> And whatsoever ye shall ask in my name, that I will do, that the father may be glorified in the son. If you ask anything in my name, I will do it. (John 14:13–14)

God will give you His grace in the midst of your loss, so press forward and fear not.

> And He said to me, my grace is sufficient for you, for My strength is made perfect in weakness. Therefore, most gladly I will rather boast in my infirmities, that the power of Christ may rest upon me. Therefore, I take pleasure in infirmities, in reproaches, in needs, in persecutions, in distresses, for Christ's sake. For when I am weak, then I am strong. (2 Corinthians 12:9–10)

An obstacle seems large when you take your eyes off the Lord, but when you call on Him, He will surely answer you, and your victory is sure in Him.

It shall come to pass that before they call, I will answer; and while they are still speaking, I will hear. (Isaiah 65:24)

And the Lord, He is the One who goes before you. He will be with you; He will not leave you nor forsake you; do not fear nor be dismayed. (Deuteronomy 31:8)

When you wait patiently on the Lord, He will fight all your battles and put a new song in your mouth.

I waited patiently for the Lord; and He inclined to me, and heard my cry. He also brought me up out of a horrible pit, out of the miry clay, and set my feet upon a rock, and established my steps. He has put a new song in my mouth—praise to our God; many will see it and fear, and will trust in the Lord. (Psalm 40:1–3)

This is the season to expect your own miracle because your God has won your battle. Trust Him. You have this hope by grace.

And he said, "Listen, all you of Judah and you inhabitants of Jerusalem, and you, King Jehoshaphat! Thus says the Lord to you: 'Do not be afraid nor dismayed because of this great multitude, for the battle is not yours, but God's.'" (2 Chronicles 20:15)

God is bigger than all your challenges. Nothing is too hard for God to handle. We cannot recreate this world, but God can. No part of your life is wasted. God is in control.

Ah, Lord God! Behold, you have made the heavens and the earth by Your great power and outstretched arm. There is nothing too hard for You. You show lovingkindness to thousands, and repay the iniquity of the fathers into the bosom of their children after them—the Great, the Mighty God, whose name is the Lord of hosts. You *are* great in counsel and mighty in work, for Your eyes are open to all the ways of the sons of men, to give everyone according to his ways and according to the fruit of his doings. (Jeremiah 32:17–19)

Life's challenges are designed not to break us but to bend us toward God. He will settle us, for His promises are sure.

But may the God of all grace, who called us to His eternal glory by Christ Jesus, after you have suffered a while, perfect, establish, strengthen, and settle you. To Him be the glory and the dominion forever and ever. Amen. (1 Peter 5:10–11)

God promises is to give you grace for every situation. He will not withhold any good thing from coming our way.

For the LORD God *is* a sun and shield; the LORD will give grace and glory; no good thing will He withhold from those who walk uprightly. O LORD of hosts, blessed is the man who trusts in You. (Psalm 84:11–12)

The Lord won't rest regarding your problems until He has won all the battles for you because His plan is to preserve you from all evil. He will never break His covenant with you.

I will lift up my eyes to the hills—from whence comes my help? My help comes from the LORD, who made heaven and earth. He will not allow your foot to be moved; He who keeps you will not slumber. Behold, He who keeps Israel shall neither slumber nor sleep. The LORD *is* your keeper; the LORD *is* your shade at your right hand. The sun shall not strike you by day, nor the moon by night. The LORD shall preserve you from all evil; He shall preserve your soul. The LORD shall preserve your going out and your coming in from this time forth, and even forevermore. (Psalm 121:1–8)

Those who see God's hand in everything can best leave everything in God's hand. So put yours there today. Your victory is sure. The empty tomb of Jesus is the foundation of our faith. Because He lives, you can face tomorrow.

> Now on the first day of the week, very early in the morning, they, and certain other women with them, came to the tomb bringing the spices which they had prepared. But they found the stone rolled away from the tomb. Then they went in and did not find the body of the Lord Jesus. And it happened, as they were greatly perplexed about this, that behold, two men stood by them in shining garments. Then, as they were afraid and bowed their faces to the earth, they said to them, "Why do you seek the living among the dead? He is not here, but is risen! Remember how He spoke to you when He was still in Galilee, saying, 'The Son of Man must be delivered into the hands of sinful men, and be crucified, and the third day rise again.'" (Luke 24:3–6)

He who drew the lines on your palms knows your trials. He will solve them one by one and will not forsake you.

> Can a woman forget her nursing child, and not have compassion on the son of her womb? Surely they may forget, yet I will not forget you. See, I have inscribed you on the palms of My hands; your walls *are* continually before Me. (Isaiah 49:15–16)

The Lord will help you to rise above despair when life's burdens seem too much to bear.

Come to Me, all *you* who labor and are heavy laden, and I will give you rest. Take My yoke upon you and learn from Me, for I am gentle and lowly in heart, and you will find rest for your souls. For My yoke *is* easy and My burden is light. (Matthew 11:28–30)

As you travel through the wilderness of life, Jesus, the living Water, will quench your thirst.

Jesus answered and said to her, "Whoever drinks of this water will thirst again, but whoever drinks of the water that I shall give him will never thirst. But the water that I shall give him will become in him a fountain of water springing up into everlasting life." (John 4:13–14)

No matter what situation you may find yourself in today, don't give up, even if the whole world—church, family, friends—give up on you. God has not given up on you. Learn to trust the turning of the seasons and the life that supports you in your journey through grief.

The righteous cry out, and the LORD hears, and delivers them out of all their troubles. The LORD is near to those who have a broken heart, and saves such as have a contrite spirit. Many *are* the afflictions of the righteous, but the LORD delivers him out of them all. (Psalm 34:17–19)

As God was with Moses, He will be with you. He will not leave you nor forsake you.

No man shall be able to stand before you all the days of your life; as I was with Moses, *so* I will be with you. I will not leave you nor forsake you. Be strong and of good courage, for to this people you shall divide as an inheritance the land which I swore to their fathers to give them. Only be strong and very courageous, that you may observe to do according to all the law which Moses My servant commanded you; do not turn from it to the right hand or to the left, that you may prosper wherever you go. (Joshua 1:5–7)

Your soul will find a resting place if you completely leave your problems in God's hand.

> When He came in, He said to them, "Why make this commotion and weep? The child is not dead, but sleeping." And they ridiculed Him. But when He had put them all outside, He took the father and the mother of the child, and those who were with Him, and entered where the child was lying. Then He took the child by the hand, and said to her, "Talitha, cumin," which is translated, "Little girl, I say to you, arise." Immediately the girl arose and walked, for she was twelve years of age. And they were overcome with great amazement. (Mark 5:39–42)

When you are in the midst of your trials and storms, you feel disturbed and fearful. A prayer of faith to God is the solution.

> But you, when you pray, go into your room, and when you have shut your door, pray to your Father who is in the secret place; and your Father who sees in secret will reward you openly. (Matthew 6:6)

When God approves your life's goals, He supplies the resources to accomplish them. In Him, your victory is sure.

> But my God shall supply all your need according to his riches in glory by Christ Jesus. Now unto God and our father be glory for ever and ever. (Philippians 4:19–20)

Whatever challenges you may be facing now, don't give up. All things will work out for your good. In God, your victory is sure.

> Trust in the Lord, and do good; dwell in the land, and feed on His faithfulness. Delight yourself also in the Lord,

and He shall give you the desires of your heart. Commit your way to the Lord, trust also in Him, and He shall bring it to pass. He shall bring forth your righteousness as the light, and your justice as the noonday. Rest in the Lord, and wait patiently for Him; do not fret because of him who prospers in his way, because of the man who brings wicked schemes to pass. Cease from anger, and forsake wrath; do not fret—it only causes harm. (Psalm 37:3–8)

Our faith in God may not be great, but our faith is in a great God who will listen and act for us. Jesus has a big shoulder to carry your burdens, so lay them down at His feet now. He will bear them for you. God who made the firmament and the deepest sea and put the stars in place is the God who will care for you.

When I consider Your heavens, the work of Your fingers, the moon and the stars, which You have ordained, what is man that You are mindful of him, and the son of man that You visit him? For You have made him a little lower than the angels, and You have crowned him with glory and honor. (Psalm 8:3–5)

Please, place your attention on God's blessing rather than on the trials of life. Don't be discouraged!

The Lord *is* merciful and gracious, slow to anger, and abounding in mercy. He will not always strive with us, nor will He keep His anger forever. He has not dealt with us according to our sins, nor punished us according to our iniquities. For as the heavens are high above the earth, so great is His mercy toward those who fear Him; as far as the east is from the west, so far has He removed our transgressions from us. As a father pities his children, so the Lord pities those who fear Him. For He knows our frame; He remembers that we are dust. (Psalm 103:8–14)

The story about the birth of Christ, which is a blessing to the world, will change your story.

> And behold, an angel of the Lord stood before them, and the glory of the Lord shone around them, and they were greatly afraid. Then the angel said to them, "Do not be afraid, for behold, I bring you good tidings of great joy which will be to all people." (Luke 2:9–10)

If God can hold the whole world in His hand, your little problem will not be too hard for Him to handle. There is a path that Jesus is planning for you. You don't need to see the way if you follow the One who is the way.

> Where can I go from Your Spirit? Or where can I flee from Your presence? If I ascend into heaven, You *are* there; if I make my bed in hell, behold, You are there. If I take the wings of the morning, *and* dwell in the uttermost parts of the sea, even there Your hand shall lead me, and Your right hand shall hold me. If I say, "Surely the darkness shall fall on me," even the night shall be light about me; indeed, the darkness shall not hide from You, but the night shines as the day; the darkness and the light *are* both alike to You. For You formed my inward parts; You covered me in my mother's womb. I will praise You, for I am fearfully *and* wonderfully made; marvelous are Your works, and that my soul knows very well. (Psalm 139:10-14)

The Lord, who numbered the hairs on your head, is able to solve all problems that may come your way.

> Are not two sparrows sold for a copper coin? And not one of them falls to the ground apart from your father's will. But the very hairs of your head are all numbered. Do not fear therefore; you are of more value than many sparrows. (Matthew 10:29–31)

Don't try to bear your trials, troubles, and temptations alone. Jesus is always by your side to help you. He knows all your woes. He will supply all your needs when in faith, you pray and trust in Him.

> Blessed is that man who makes the LORD his trust, and does not respect the proud, nor such as turn aside to lies. Many, O LORD my God, *are* Your wonderful works which You have done; and Your thoughts toward us cannot be recounted to You in order; if I would declare and speak of them, they are more than can be numbered.
> (Psalm 40:4–5)

God remains faithful to His promises. This assurance is in our hearts, and the timing is in His hand.

> And the LORD visited Sarah as He had said, and the LORD did for Sarah as He had spoken. For Sarah conceived and bore Abraham a son in his old age, at the set time of which God had spoken to him. And Abraham called the name of his son who was born to him—whom Sarah bore to him—Isaac. (Genesis 21:1–3)

Place your concerns in the capable hand of God, and you will find quietness that only He can provide.

> Be still, and know that I am God; I will be exalted among the nations, I will be exalted in the earth! The LORD of hosts is with us; the God of Jacob is our refuge.
> (Psalm 46:10–11)

Let your faith be strong in the Lord like Israel of old when they crossed Jordan River.

> And Joshua said to the people, "Sanctify yourselves, for tomorrow the LORD will do wonders among you.
> (Joshua 3:5)

Are you feeling anxious and afraid about your life? Don't be afraid because God has everything under control.

> Fear not, for I am with you; be not dismayed, for I am your God. I will strengthen you, yes, I will help you, I will uphold you with My righteous right hand. (Isaiah 41:10)

Keep your faith in God like Abraham of old, and God will fulfil His promise and come to your aid.

> Then Abraham fell upon his face, and laughed, and said in his heart, Shall a child be born unto him that is an hundred years old? and shall Sarah, that is ninety years old, bear? And Abraham said unto God, O that Ishmael might live before thee! And God said, Sarah thy wife shall bear thee a son indeed; and thou shalt call his name Isaac: and I will establish my covenant with him for an everlasting covenant, and with his seed after him. (Genesis 18:17–19)

Faith works. Your days will be filled with the manifestation of God's glory in your life. His presence shall guild you night and day. Your victory is sure!

> The LORD will guide you continually, and satisfy your soul in drought, and strengthen your bones; you shall be like a watered garden, and like a spring of water, whose waters do not fail. (Isaiah 58:11)

Faith works. Mordecai and Israel overcame the plots of Haman. Rejoice in the Lord, for you shall overcome all the obstacles that come your way. Your victory is sure!

> So Haman took the robe and the horse, arrayed Mordecai and led him on horseback through the city square, and proclaimed before him, "Thus shall it be done to the man whom the king delights to honor!" Afterward Mordecai

went back to the king's gate. But Haman hurried to his
house, mourning and with his head covered. When Haman
told his wife Zeresh and all his friends everything that had
happened to him, his wise men and his wife Zeresh said to
him, "If Mordecai, before whom you have begun to fall,
is of Jewish descent, you will not prevail against him but
will surely fall before him." (Esther 6:11–12)

And we know that all things work together for good
to those who love God, to those who are the called
according to His purpose. For whom He foreknew, He
also predestined to be conformed to the image of His Son,
that He might be the firstborn among many brethren.
(Romans 8:28–29)

From whom the whole family in heaven and earth is
named, that He would grant you, according to the riches
of His glory, to be strengthened with might through His
Spirit in the inner man, that Christ may dwell in your
hearts through faith; that you, being rooted and grounded
in love, may be able to comprehend with all the saints
what *is* the width and length and depth and height to
know the love of Christ which passes knowledge; that you
may be filled with all the fullness of God.
(Ephesians 3:15–19)

Faith works. All the dreams of Joseph were manifested. All your
dreams and expectations shall come to pass by the grace of God almighty.
Your victory is sure!

Then he dreamed still another dream and told it to his
brothers, and said, "Look, I have dreamed another dream.
And this time, the sun, the moon, and the eleven stars
bowed down to me." (Genesis 37:9)

We can agree that we are quite flawed—beautiful but broken and spirited but sinful. We don't always work right. God is not shocked that we don't work well and that we are sometimes jealous, hurtful, rude, deceitful, too much of something, and not enough of something else. God still loves us the way we are.

Chapter 3

GOD'S WORD FOR COMFORT

Have the mindset that neither your past nor your future can weigh you down. Only the present can do this. The present will shrink to littleness if you set its boundaries. The present sorrow is often difficult for us to deal with, the past is over, and the future is unknown. Limit your concerns to this day only.

> Blessed are those who mourn, for they shall be comforted.
> (Matthew 5:4)

God will deliver you from all the arrows of the enemy. He will preserve you for His glory. He will heal you from all your fears. You will become stronger in the Lord and hidden from terror by Him. God will cover you with His wings. Your family shall be safe from enemies. In God, your victory is sure!

> And Moses said to the people, "Do not be afraid. Standstill, and see the salvation of the LORD, which He will accomplish for you today. For the Egyptians whom you see today, you shall see again no more forever. The LORD will fight for you, and you shall hold your peace." (Exodus 14:13–14)

There is no battle of life that our God cannot win. He will fight for you if you trust Him.

> Who *is* like You, O LORD, among the gods? Who *is* like You, glorious in holiness, fearful in praises, doing wonders? You stretched out Your right hand; the earth swallowed them. You in Your mercy have led forth the people whom You have redeemed; You have guided them in Your strength to Your holy habitation. (Exodus 15:11–13)

Do not be afraid, for you will not suffer or face humiliation. God will not give you as prey to your enemies. Your victory is sure in Him. The harassment of the enemy is nothing when God is in your camp. He will defend and fight your battle.

> Therefore, thus says the LORD concerning the king of Assyria: "He shall not come into this city, nor shoot an arrow there nor come before it with shield, nor build a siege mound against it. By the way that he came, by the same shall he return; and he shall not come into this city," says the LORD. "For I will defend this city, to save it for My own sake and for My servant David's sake." (Isaiah 37:33–35)

As a lily pushes its way through hard soil and thrives in beauty and glory amidst thorns, you will also excel and prosper beyond every limiting wall, so fear not! As God shut the mouth of the lions on behalf of Daniel, He will do the same for you. He will fight for you, so trust, obey, and have faith in Him.

> Then the king arose very early in the morning and went in haste to the den of lions. And when he came to the den, he cried out with a lamenting voice to Daniel. The king spoke, saying to Daniel, "Daniel, servant of the living God, has your God, whom you serve continually, been able to deliver you from the lions?" Then Daniel said to the king, "O king, live forever! My God sent His angel

and shut the lions' mouths, so that they have not hurt me, because I was found innocent before Him; and also, O king, I have done no wrong before you." Now the king was exceedingly glad for him, and commanded that they should take Daniel up out of the den. So, Daniel was taken up out of the den, and no injury whatever was found on him, because he believed in his God. (Daniel 6:19–23)

God will dismantle depression, frustration, and the hindrances of the enemy in your life, and you will rejoice. Whatever you are going through, don't make enemies; pray for them.

You have heard that it was said, "You shall love your neighbor and hate your enemy." But I say to you, love your enemies, bless those who curse you, do good to those who hate you, and pray for those who spitefully use you and persecute you, that you may be sons of your Father in heaven; for He makes His sun rise on the evil and on the good, and sends rain on the just and on the unjust. (Matthew 5:43–46)

He who says he is in the light, and hates his brother, is in darkness until now. He who loves his brother abides in the light, and there is no cause for stumbling in him. But he who hates his brother is in darkness and walks in darkness, and does not know where he is going, because the darkness has blinded his eyes. (1 John 2:9–11)

You remain God's chosen generation despite your shortcomings.

But you are a chosen generation, a royal priesthood, a holy nation, His own special people, that you may proclaim the praises of Him who called you out of darkness into His marvelous light who once were not a people but are now the people of God, who had not obtained mercy but now have obtained mercy. (1 Peter 2:9–10)

Chapter 4

GOD'S WORD FOR NEEDS

God knows your heart, He sees your struggles and needs, and He's aware of your weaknesses. And He's right there in the midst of your anxieties, fears, and needs.

> Therefore, I say unto you, do not worry about your life, what you will eat or what you will drink; nor about your body, what you will put on. Is not life more than food and the body more than clothing? Look at the birds of the air, for they neither sow nor reap nor gather into barns; yet your heavenly Father feeds them. Are you not of more value than they? Which of you by worrying can add one cubit to his stature? So why do you worry about clothing? Consider the lilies of the field, how they grow: they neither toil nor spin; and yet I say to you that even Solomon in all his glory was not arrayed like one of these. Now if God so clothes the grass of the field, which today is, and tomorrow is thrown into the oven, will He not much more clothe you, O you of little faith? Therefore, do not worry, saying, "What shall we eat?" or "What shall we drink?" or "What shall we wear?" For after all these things the Gentiles seek. For your heavenly Father knows that you need all these things. But seek first the kingdom of God and His

righteousness, and all these things shall be added to you. Therefore, do not worry about tomorrow, for tomorrow will worry about its own things. Sufficient for the day is its own trouble. (Matthew 6:25–34)

God met Abraham's need on Mount Moriah. He will provide for you, henceforth, claim this in faith because you have this hope by grace.

And in that day, you will ask Me nothing. Most assuredly, I say to you, whatever you ask the Father in My name He will give you. Until now you have asked nothing in My name. Ask, and you will receive, that your joy may be full. (John 16:23–24)

Let us therefore come boldly to the throne of grace, that we may obtain mercy and find grace to help in time of need. (Hebrews 4:16)

God has more than enough for everyone. Your needs will never exhaust God's supply, so trust in Him.

I know all fowls of the mountains: and the wild beasts of the field are mine. If I were hungry, I would not tell thee: for the world is mine and the fullness thereof. Offer to God thanksgiving, and pay your vows to the Most High. Call upon Me in the day of trouble; I will deliver you, and you shall glorify me. (Psalm 50:13–15)

The God who met the needs of Elijah when he was in a wilderness cave and under the juniper tree, hungry, fearful, and thirsty, will also provide for your needs.

Then as he lay and slept under a broom tree, suddenly an angel touched him, and said to him, "Arise and eat." Then he looked, and there by his head *was* a cake baked on coals, and a jar of water. So, he ate and drank, and lay down again. And the angel of the LORD came back the second time, and touched him, and said, "Arise *and* eat, because the journey *is* too great for you." So, he arose, and ate and drank; and he went in the strength of that food forty days and forty nights as far as Horeb, the mountain of God. (1 King 19:3–8)

The God who provided for the widow of Zarephath when all hope was lost, and there seemed no way out will surely provide for your needs more than you can imagine. God is a God of possibilities.

Elijah said to her, "Do not fear; go and do as you have said, but make me a small cake from it first, and bring *it* to me; and afterward make some for yourself and your son. For thus says the LORD God of Israel: 'The bin of flour shall not be used up, nor shall the jar of oil run dry, until the day the LORD sends rain on the earth.'" So, she went away and did according to the word of Elijah; and she and he and her household ate for many days. The bin of flour was not used up, nor did the jar of oil run dry, according to the word of the LORD which He spoke by Elijah. (1 King 17:13–16)

Are you feeling tense about your future? Remember that God is always present. He will grant grace for each day, each week, each month, and each year of your life.

As God listened to the solemn prayer of Mary, granted the request of Elijah for rain, and answered Hannah's sincere prayer for a son, in His love, God will be attentive to your supplications this day, month, and year. Your victory is sure in Him.

The LORD makes poor and makes rich; He brings low and lifts up. He raises the poor from the dust *and* lifts the beggar from the ash heap, to set them among princes and make them inherit the throne of glory. For the pillars of the earth are the LORD's, and He has set the world upon

them. He will guard the feet of His saints, but the wicked shall be silent in darkness.
(1 Samuel 2:7–9)

Therefore, my beloved, as you have always obeyed, not as in my presence only, but now much more in my absence, work out your own salvation with fear and trembling; for it is God who works in you both to will and to do for *His* good pleasure. (Philippians 2:12–13)

"If any little word of mine may make a life the brighter
If any little of mine may make a heart the lighter
God help me speak the little word and take my bit of singing
And drop it in some lovely vale to set the echoes ringing.
If any little love of mine may make a life the sweeter
If any little care of mine may make a friend's heart's the fleeter
If any little lift of mine may ease the burden of another
God give me love and care and strength to help my needy sister and my brother".
("If Any Little Word of Mine," written by Connie Vanderman Jeffery,)[A4R3]

Chapter 5
God's Word for Hope

Life can be difficult sometimes. All of us go through seasons filled with difficulty, grief, or loss. And even if you haven't experienced those things yet, you've probably had moments where you've grown tired of doing good. As much as we want to live well and do good to others, the truth is that we will all grow weary of it at some point. But those who hope in God will find renewed strength. The key to perseverance in difficult seasons is not simply pushing through and trying harder. Strength isn't found in simply hoping our circumstances will change. God's Word says that true strength comes from placing our hope in God. Because God is all-powerful, He alone has the power to change our circumstances. But God also knows that as humans, we grow weary and restless. We often place our hope in temporary solutions when we should be relying on God, who can truly help us.

But when we place our hope in God alone, scripture tells us that we will find renewed strength to endure life's challenges. Hoping in God means trusting in His promises—even if we don't see them fulfilled in our lifetimes. Pray that you will be filled with the strength and hope that only God can provide.

> Hast thou not known? Hast thou not heard, that the everlasting God, the LORD, the Creator of the ends of the earth, fainted not, neither is weary? There is no searching of his understanding.

He giveth power to the faint; and to them that have no might he increased strength. Even the youths shall faint and be weary, and the young men shall utterly fall: But they that wait upon the LORD shall renew their strength; they shall mount up with wings as eagles; they shall run, and not be weary; and they shall walk, and not faint. (Isaiah 40:28–31)

May each step you take every day draw you closer to God and fill any emptiness in your life. Like the Samaritan woman at the well, your victory is sure in the Lord.

Blessed be the Lord, who daily loads us with benefits, the God of our salvation! (Psalm 68:19)

But whoever drinks of the water that I shall give him will never thirst. But the water that I shall give him will become in him a fountain of water springing up into everlasting life. (John 4:14)

Through the prophet Isaiah, the Lord God says to you this day that every valley in your life will be exalted, every mountain and hill shall be made low, the crooked ways in your life shall be made straight, and the rough places of life will be made plain. The glory of the Lord will be revealed in your life, family, home, and community. Claim God's promises, His mouth has spoken.

Every valley shall be exalted and every mountain and hill brought low; the crooked places shall be made straight and the rough places smooth; the glory of the LORD shall be revealed, and all flesh shall see *it* together; for the mouth of the LORD has spoken. (Isaiah 40:4–5)

God has spoken that for all your days, all the issues in your life shall receive divine intervention.

"He will bring forth justice for truth. He will not fail nor be discouraged, till He has established justice in the earth; and the coastlands shall wait for His law." Thus says God the LORD, who created the heavens and stretched them out, who spread forth the earth and that which comes from it, who gives breath to the people on it, and spirit to those who walk on it: "I, the LORD, have called You in righteousness, and will hold Your hand; I will keep You and give You as a covenant to the people, as a light to the Gentiles." (Isaiah 42:4–6)

I thank God for being the Lawgiver who came to Earth to redeem lawbreakers.

And she will bring forth a Son, and you shall call His name JESUS, for He will save His people from their sins. (Matthew1:21)

God will cancel every plot, plan, and scheme that the devil has devised against you.

"No weapon formed against you shall prosper, and every tongue which rises against you in judgment You shall condemn. This *is* the heritage of the servants of the LORD, and their righteousness *is* from Me," says the LORD. (Isaiah 54:17)

Should you face heartaches or trials, trust God. Our God will bring a better day for you.

Now the LORD blessed the latter days of Job more than his beginning; for he had fourteen thousand sheep, six thousand camels, one thousand yoke of oxen, and one thousand female donkeys. He also had seven sons and three daughters. (Job 42:12–13)

Lay your burdens down at the feet of the Lord. He will bear them for you. Your victory in Him is sure.

> Come to Me, all *you* who labor and are heavy laden, and I will give you rest. Take My yoke upon you and learn from Me, for I am gentle and lowly in heart, and you will find rest for your souls. For My yoke *is* easy and My burden is light. (Mathew 11:28–30)

God, the I am that I am, will certainly be with you throughout your years. Your Red Sea will depart so that you can move on.

> And God said to Moses, "I AM WHO I AM." And He said, "Thus you shall say to the children of Israel, 'I AM has sent me to you.' " Moreover, God said to Moses, "Thus you shall say to the children of Israel: 'The LORD God of your fathers, the God of Abraham, the God of Isaac, and the God of Jacob, has sent me to you. This *is* My name forever, and this *is* My memorial to all generations (Exodus 3:14–15)

Chapter 6

GOD'S WORD OF PEACE

Peace, I leave with you, my peace I give to you; not as the world gives do I give to you. Let not your heart be troubled, neither let it be afraid.
—John: 14: 27

Salt *is* good, but if the salt loses its flavor, how will you season it? Have salt in yourselves, and have peace with one another.
—Mark 9:50

He Himself is our peace, who has made both one, and has broken down the middle wall of separation, having abolished in His flesh the enmity, that is, the law of commandments contained in ordinances, so as to create in Himself one new man *from* the two, *thus* making peace, and that He might reconcile them both to God in one body through the cross, thereby putting to death the enmity. And He came and preached peace to you who were afar off and to those who were near. For through Him we both have access by one Spirit to the Father.
—Ephesians 2:14–18

Obey all God's commandments, and it shall be well with you.

> But showing mercy to thousands, to those who love Me and keep My commandments. (Exodus 20:6)

> Oh, that you had heeded My commandments! Then your peace would have been like a river, and your righteousness like the waves of the sea. (Isaiah 48:18)

By faith, we can move our mountains.

> Therefore, having been justified by faith, we have peace with God through our Lord Jesus Christ, through whom also we have access by faith into this grace in which we stand, and rejoice in hope of the glory of God. And not only that, but we also glory in tribulations, knowing that tribulation produces perseverance; and perseverance, character; and character, hope. Now hope does not disappoint, because the love of God has been poured out in our hearts by the Holy Spirit who was given to us. (Romans 5:1–5)

The peace of God rules in your heart.

> And let the peace of God rule in your hearts, to which also you were called in one body; and be thankful. Let the word of Christ dwell in you richly in all wisdom, teaching and admonishing one another in psalms and hymns and spiritual songs, singing with grace in your hearts to the Lord. And whatever you do in word or deed, do all in the name of the Lord Jesus, giving thanks to God the Father through Him. (Colossians 3:15–17)

> Therefore we also, since we are surrounded by so great a cloud of witnesses, let us lay aside every weight, and the sin which so easily ensnares us, and let us run with endurance the race that is set before us, looking unto

Jesus, the author and finisher of our faith, who for the joy that was set before Him endured the cross, despising the shame, and has sat down at the right hand of the throne of God. (Hebrews 12:1–2)

Brethren, whatever things are true, whatever things are noble, whatever things are just, whatever things are pure, whatever things are lovely, whatever things *are* of good report, if there is any virtue and if there is anything praiseworthy—meditate on these things. The things which you learned and received and heard and saw in me, these do, and the God of peace will be with you. (Philippians 4:8–9)

Now may the Lord of peace Himself give you peace always in every way. The Lord be with you all. (2 Thessalonians 3:16)

Chapter 7

GOD'S WORD FOR HEALING

We are healed of a suffering only by experiencing it to
the full.
—Marcel Prius

But He was wounded for our transgressions, He was
bruised for our iniquities; the chastisement for our peace
was upon Him, and by His stripes we are healed.
—Isaiah 53:5

Obey God's commandments and statutes, and all shall be well with you!

If you diligently heed the voice of the LORD your God and
do what is right in His sight, give ear to His commandments
and keep all His statutes, I will put none of the diseases
on you which I have brought on the Egyptians. For I am
the LORD who heals you. (Exodus 15:26)

Have mercy on me, O LORD, for I am weak; O LORD, heal
me, for my bones are troubled. (Psalm 6:2)

The healer of yesterday is the same healer today and tomorrow. Jesus
remains the same. Seek Him and claim His healing over you!

And the prayer of faith will save the sick, and the Lord will raise him up. And if he has committed sins, he will be forgiven. Confess your trespasses to one another, and pray for one another, that you may be healed. The effective, fervent prayer of a righteous man avails much. (James 5:15–16)

And Jesus went about all Galilee, teaching in their synagogues, preaching the gospel of the kingdom, and healing all kinds of sickness and all kinds of disease among the people. Then His fame went throughout all Syria; and they brought to Him all sick people who were afflicted with various diseases and torments, and those who were demon-possessed, epileptics, and paralytics; and He healed them. Great multitudes followed Him— from Galilee, and from Decapolis, Jerusalem, Judea, and beyond the Jordan. (Matthew 4:25)

The promised hope of eternity is real. We have the real deal of healing and eternal life.

In the middle of its street, and on either side of the river, was the tree of life, which bore twelve fruits, each tree yielding its fruit every month. The leaves of the tree were for the healing of the nations. And there shall be no more curse, but the throne of God and of the Lamb shall be in it, and His servants shall serve Him. They shall see His face, and His name shall be on their foreheads. There shall be no night there: They need no lamp nor light of the sun, for the Lord God gives them light. And they shall reign forever and ever. (Revelation 22:2–5)

Chapter 8

GOD'S WORD FOR REFUGE

May the Lord remain your refuge and strong tower against all foes. No arrow of the evil one shall reach your home.

He who dwells in the secret place of the Most High shall abide under the shadow of the Almighty. I will say of the LORD, "He is my refuge and my fortress; my God, in Him I will trust." Surely He shall deliver you from the snare of the fowler and from the perilous pestilence. He shall cover you with His feathers, and under His wings you shall take refuge; His truth shall be your shield and buckler. You shall not be afraid of the terror by night, nor of the arrow *that* flies by day, nor of the pestilence *that* walks in darkness, nor of the destruction that lays waste at noonday. A thousand may fall at your side, and ten thousand at your right hand; but it shall not come near you. Only with your eyes shall you look, and see the reward of the wicked. Because you have made the LORD, who *is* my refuge, even the Most High, your dwelling place, no evil shall befall you, nor shall any plague come near your dwelling; for He shall give His angels charge over you, to keep you in all your ways. In their hands they shall bear you up, lest you dash your foot against a stone.

You shall tread upon the lion and the cobra, the young lion and the serpent you shall trample underfoot.

Because he has set his love upon Me, therefore I will deliver him; I will set him on high, because he has known My name. He shall call upon Me, and I will answer him; I will be with him in trouble; I will deliver him and honor him. With long life I will satisfy him, and show him My salvation. (Psalm 91:1–16)

"God is our refuge and strength, a very present help in trouble. Therefore we will not fear, even though the earth be removed, and though the mountains be carried into the midst of the sea; Though its waters roar *and* be troubled, though the mountains shake with its swelling. (Psalm 46:1–3)

The Lord who made a way for Israel of old will surely come to your rescue.

And Moses said to the people, "Do not be afraid. Standstill, and see the salvation of the LORD, which He will accomplish for you today. For the Egyptians whom you see today, you shall see again no more forever. The LORD will fight for you, and you shall hold your peace. (Exodus 14:13–14)

God is our Deliverer. If you depend on Him for everything, you overcome anything, and your victory is sure.

O Death, where *is* your sting? O Hades, where *is* your victory? The sting of death *is* sin, and the strength of sin is the law. But thanks be to God, who gives us the victory through our Lord Jesus Christ. Therefore, my beloved brethren, be steadfast, immovable, always abounding in the work of the Lord, knowing that your labor is not in vain in the Lord. (1 Corinthians 15:55–58)

There is no battle of life that our God cannot win. He will fight for you if you trust Him. Pray for an unfaltering faith that stands strong because great faith is often built during great trials.

> Whatever I tell you in the dark, speak in the light; and what you hear in the ear, preach on the housetops. And do not fear those who kill the body but cannot kill the soul. But rather fear Him who is able to destroy both soul and body. (Matthew 10:27–29)

God said the battles of your life are His, so don't be dismayed. Just follow His plan.

> And he said, "Listen, all you of Judah and you inhabitants of Jerusalem, and you, King Jehoshaphat! Thus says the LORD to you: 'Do not be afraid nor dismayed because of this great multitude, for the battle *is* not yours, but God's.'" (2 Chronicles 20:15)

> Blessed be the LORD, who has not given us *as* prey to their teeth. Our soul has escaped as a bird from the snare of the fowlers; the snare is broken, and we have escaped. Our help *is* in the name of the LORD, who made heaven and earth. (Psalm 124:6–8)

No one is temptation immune. The only way to overcome is by focusing on Jesus, who never fails.

> Therefore, we also, since we are surrounded by so great a cloud of witnesses, let us lay aside every weight, and the sin which so easily ensnares *us,* and let us run with endurance the race that is set before us, looking unto Jesus, the author and finisher of our faith, who for the joy that was set before Him endured the cross, despising the shame, and has sat down at the right hand of the throne of God. (Hebrew 12:1–2)

When Jesus entered Zacchaeus's home, Zacchaeus was redeemed. Jesus will restore your lost glory.

> And when Jesus came to the place, He looked up and saw him, and said to him, "Zacchaeus, make haste and come down, for today I must stay at your house." So he made haste and came down, and received Him joyfully. But when they saw *it*, they all complained, saying, "He has gone to be a guest with a man who is a sinner." Then Zacchaeus stood and said to the Lord, "Look, Lord, I give half of my goods to the poor; and if I have taken anything from anyone by false accusation, I restore fourfold." And Jesus said to him, "Today salvation has come to this house, because he also is a son of Abraham; for the Son of Man has come to seek and to save that which was lost." (Luke 19:5–10)

> The Lord is my shepherd; I shall not want. He makes me to lie down in green pastures; He leads me beside the still waters. He restores my soul; He leads me in the paths of righteousness for His name's sake. Yea, though I walk through the valley of the shadow of death, I will fear no evil; For You are with me; Your rod and Your staff, they comfort me. You prepare a table before me in the presence of my enemies; You anoint my head with oil; my cup runs over. Surely goodness and mercy shall follow me all the days of my life; and I will dwell in the house of the Lord forever. (Psalm 23:1–6)

The Gospel Truth

"The Fellowship of the Unashamed"

"I have Holy Spirit power. The die has been cast.

I have stepped over the line. I have put my hands to the plough, The decision has been made. I am a disciple of Jesus Christ. I will not look back, let up, slow down, back away or be still. My past is redeemed, my present makes sense and my future is secure. I am finished and done with low living, sight walking, small planning, smooth Knees, colorless dreams, tamed visions, mundane talking, meager giving and dwarfed goals!

I no longer need prominence, prosperity, position, promotion, praise or popularity. I don't have to be right, be first, be tops, respected, recognized, praised, regarded, or rewarded. I now live by faith, lean on his presence, walk with patience, live by prayer, labor With power, and honor with obedience and speak in love. My face is set like flint, my pace is fast, and my goal is heaven. My road is narrow, my way is rough, and my companions are few.

My Guild is reliable, my mission clear. I cannot be bought, compromised, detoured, lured away, threatened, Intimidated, manipulated, turned back, deluded, or delayed. I will not flinch in the face of sacrifice; hesitate in the presence of the adversary, negotiate at the table of the enemy, ponder at the pool of popularity or meander in the maze of mediocrity or wade in the sea of sin, I will not give up or let up until I have stayed up, stored up, Prayed up, paid up and preached up the cause of Christ!

I must go until He comes, give till I drop, preach till all know and work till He stops me. And when He comes for me, He will have no problem recognizing me; my colors will be clear, my banner will be clean, my treasure will be laid up, and my faith will endure"
by H.B Charles Jr. [B6]

Cast Down but Unconquered

But we have this treasure in earthen vessels, that the excellence of the power may be of God and not of us. We are hard-pressed on every side, yet not crushed; we are perplexed, but not in despair; persecuted, but not forsaken; struck down, but not destroyed— always carrying about in the body the dying of the Lord Jesus, that the life of Jesus also may be manifested in our body. For we who live are always delivered to death for Jesus' sake, that the life of Jesus also may be manifested in our mortal flesh. So, then death is working in us, but life in you.
(2 Corinthians 4:7–12)

There hath no temptation taken you but such as is common to man: but God is faithful, who will not suffer you to be tempted above that ye are able; but will with the temptation also make a way to escape, that ye may be able to bear it. (1 Corinthians 10:13)

Seeing the Invisible

Therefore, we do not lose heart. Even though our outward man is perishing, yet the inward man is being renewed day by day. For our light affliction, which is but for a moment, is working for us a far more exceeding and eternal weight of glory, while we do not look at the things which are seen, but at the things which are not seen. For the things which are seen are temporary, but the things which are not seen are eternal. (2 Corinthians 4:16–18)

Let us therefore come boldly to the throne of grace, that we may obtain mercy and find grace to help in time of need. (Hebrew 4:16)

O God, You are our help in ages past, our hope for years to come, our shelter from the stormy blast, and our eternal home. Be our guide while life lasts and our eternal home!

Prayer

Lord, I am awe of You. The problems of this world can be frightening, but You are greater than my problems. I'm so grateful I can always count on You. Your will is perfect, and Your plans are good. Your power is perfected in my weakness, and it is greater than any situation I might face. I thank You for showing me your faithfulness every day. In Jesus's name, I pray. Amen.

Conclusion

God, thank You that You are with us in **the** struggle **and** that we are never alone. You are with us in what is painful, sad, terrifying, and real. Thank You for not being far away, unavailable, or shaming about our pain, loss, struggle, weaknesses, and insecurit**ies**. Thank You for knowing pain **and** choosing to walk through it and not under or around it. **Thank You** for **teach**ing us **what** we need to learn about pain and loss. Thank You for being for us; if You made us, You are for us. If You came to Earth to be with us, You are for us. Help us, God, in our weakness, loss, and pain. Amen.

These things I have spoken unto you, that in me ye might have peace. In the world ye shall have tribulation: but be of good cheer; I have overcome the world. (John 16:33)

Is there anything happening round you that makes you feel anxious or afraid? Take note of those things and then imagine Jesus speaking this verse over you and your circumstances. Take any of your requests or concerns to Him in prayer. Abide in Him and trust His leading in all of your circumstances.

Notes

Chapter 1

1. Walter Stillman Martin, "God Will Take Care of You," Religious Hymns and Gospel Songs (1935), https://en.wikipedia.org/wiki/Walter_Stillman_MartinText under CC-BY-SA license.
2. Henri Nouwen, "A Life of the Beloved" *A-Z Quotes,* https://www.azquotes.com/author/10905-He....

Chapter 4

3. Connie Vanderman Jeffery, "If Any Little Word of Mine," *It Is written* (July16, 2021), adventistfaith.com https://www.adventistfaith.com/about/staff.
4. Martha Whitmore Hickman, "Daily Meditation for Working through Grief," https://www.audible.com.
5. Max Lucado, *"You'll Get through This,"* https://www.christianbook.com
6. H.B Charles Jr., "The Fellowship of the Unashamed", *The Gospel Truth, (Jul 30,2008)* The Fellowship of the Unashamed · H.B. Charles Jr. (hbcharlesjr.com)

Printed in the United States
by Baker & Taylor Publisher Services